LETTERS TO
HARRY BAINBRIDGE

Frederick William
ROLFE
BARON CORVO

★

Letters to
HARRY BAINBRIDGE

Edited with an Introduction by
MIRIAM J. BENKOVITZ

LONDON/ENITHARMON PRESS/1977

First published in 1976
by the Enitharmon Press
22 Huntingdon Road
East Finchley London N2 9DU

The Enitharmon Press
acknowledges financial assistance from the
Arts Council of Great Britain

SBN 901111 95 3

*Printed and made in Great Britain
by Skelton's Press Wellingborough
Northants*

CONTENTS

To

DOROTHY BETHURUM LOOMIS

INTRODUCTION by MIRIAM J. BENKOVITZ

AT one time or another, Harry Bainbridge was the associate of Dr. Ludwig Mond, genius of industrial metals; Carl Fabergé, genius of another kind of metals, enamelled and set with gems; the Rothschilds (especially Leopold) and Sir Ernest Cassel, geniuses of finance; as well as crowned heads, male and female: kings and queens of Portugal, Norway, Greece, Denmark, and above all England. Yet Bainbridge declared that 'the most baffling and exciting personality who ever lived' was the man who called himself Baron Corvo, Frederick William Rolfe.

Bainbridge was twenty-five and Rolfe thirty-nine when they first met in August 1899. Rolfe, former schoolmaster, failed priest, unsuccessful painter and photographer, and recently an inmate of the Holywell workhouse, had come to London in February, determined to make his way and his name as a writer. He had already got a start with the publication most notably of six 'Toto Stories' first in several numbers of John Lane's *Yellow Book* and then, revised, in *Stories Toto Told Me*. He was currently at work on another set of stories, also for John Lane. Acting sometimes as an agent in these transactions and sometimes as a convenience-address, was Edward Slaughter, solicitor. For a brief time in 1886, Rolfe had tutored him when Slaughter, then fifteen, was too ill to be at school. Since 1896 or '97, Slaughter, by that time a partner in his father's firm, Slaughter and Colgrave Solicitors, had acted for Rolfe. The two men also had some agreement whereby Slaughter provided Rolfe with a small, regular income to be returned from the sale of Rolfe's work.

Slaughter made the introduction to Bainbridge. They were both lodgers in the home of Mrs. Isabelle Griffiths at 69 Broadhurst Gardens, Hampstead. That evening in August 1899, Slaughter wanted to go to Confession, and he asked Bainbridge to look after a visitor. The visitor, 'a muffler round his neck—he had no collar—and carpet slippers on his feet, spectacles over his eagle eyes,' was Rolfe. Bainbridge welcomed him but went on idly playing Tchaikowsky (Rolfe later referred to the piece as 'Chant sans Paroles') while Rolfe sat down and,

as soon as he had rolled his cigarette with quick, sure move-
ments, began to smoke. When Bainbridge tired of his music,
he entertained his guest by reading aloud from a piece in *The
Wide World Magazine* which had captured his imagination,
'How I Was Buried Alive.' Bainbridge finished, and Rolfe, who
was still smoking, declared, 'I wrote it.' Bainbridge confirmed
the statement by comparing the photograph at the head of the
article with Rolfe. They then talked until Slaughter reclaimed
his visitor and took him from Bainbridge's room into his own.

A week or so later, Bainbridge received the first of the
thirty-four letters published here. Of these, thirty-two plus the
Appendix are in Rolfe's holograph. They are laid down in a
brown leatherette loose leaf album, which is a part of the Martyr
Worthy Collection. Although Bainbridge published several of
the letters or parts of them in *Twice Seven* (London: George
Routledge & Sons, Ltd., 1933), the texts are transcribed from
the holographs. The order of the undated letters in the album
has been changed here, a fact indicated in the notes. The texts
of the two letters which are not in the Martyr Worthy Collection
come from *Twice Seven*, pp. 112-14, 101-02. In no letter has
anything been changed, omitted, or added, except unimportant
punctuation marks and parts of addresses and dates.

Rolfe's letters to Bainbridge do not demonstrate the
charismatic charm which Bainbridge attributed to Rolfe.
Except for the letter of 31 December 1901, they lack the wit
and exuberant imagination on the one hand and the gleeful,
satirical quarrelsomeness on the other of a number of his letters.
These letters to Bainbridge, however, give an account of Rolfe's
difficult, lonely life during the period of his greatest effort to
earn his way by writing. They show him in tatters, penniless,
frantically trying to keep a roof over his head and to do his work.
They suggest as well an unexpected relationship with a woman,
his landlady, Mrs. Griffiths. It had its ups and downs, and
eventually she put him out; but it was characterized on Rolfe's
part by consideration, dependence, and helplessness before
Mrs. Griffiths's anger, although he was careful to deny the
'ordinary liasons or vices.'

The letters end for no apparent reason. Contrary to Rolfe's
reputation for ingratitude, for turning against those who

befriended him, Rolfe demonstrates here that he was capable of a sustained friendship without its terminating in self-justification or bitter recriminations. Harry Bainbridge said that he never saw Rolfe again after the letter of 28 September 1903. But obviously the letters went on even though Rolfe, absorbed in *Nicholas Crabbe* (London: Chatto & Windus, 1958), a new book on which he was at work, preferred to see no one. In any case, Bainbridge and Rolfe had nothing more to say to each other; so the correspondence ended.

For help of various kinds, acknowledgments are due especially to Winifred A. Myers; John and Martin Roth, owners of the Martyr Worthy Collection formed by their father the late David Roth; George F. Sims; Barbara Smith of Skidmore College Library; W. J. Smith, Head Archivist of the Greater London Council; Julian Symons, who gave permission for publication; and the late Mary E. Williams.

MIRIAM J. BENKOVITZ

Skidmore College
July 1975

THE LETTERS

I

2^A *Marlborough Rd,*
Bedford Park, W.1.

DEAR BAINBRIDGE,

While Slaughter's[2] away, I wish you would invite me to stay with you; because I'm stony broke.

My book[3] *must* be finished at once without delay.

Davis[4] puts me up till Thursday and I'm writing all the time.

On Friday, he has some other visitors coming, and I shall have to turn out. I've no money to go anywhere and that will be fatal to my book.

So I wish you'd ask me to stay with you.

I only want to sit tight

,, ,,   ,,   ,, ,,   ,,   and write

,, ,,   ,,   ,, ,,   ,,   ,,   ,,   morning noon & night.

Vty

CORVO

Meanwhile something may turn up & Davis will be free later.

I

¹ The letter is written on the letter head of the Hogarth Club, 175 Bond Street, W.1. Rolfe has scored the heading. The Hogarth Club, founded in 1870, was a rendezvous in 1899 for writers, publishers, artists of all *métiers*. Rolfe was a member, but he used the club primarily as a postal address. The Hogarth Club ceased to exist in 1900.

² Edward Joseph Slaughter (1872-1954). See the *Introduction* above. Slaughter figures as Neddy Carnage in Rolfe's *Nicholas Crabbe*, London: Chatto & Windus, 1958.

³ *In His Own Image*. London and New York: John Lane: The Bodley Head, 1901. Rolfe has drawn three vertical lines by 'My' for emphasis.

⁴ Probably William Henry Davis, a chartered accountant.

II

Hogarth Club,
175 Bond St, W.
Sept. xviiii. 1899.[1]

DEAR BAINBRIDGE,

Trousers arrived safely. Many thanks. Man without trousers is, after all, but a poor class of thing.

The rosary was in the pocket.

Davis had given me that lovely amber one which I coveted; but mine has more value, for it has at least 5000 years indulgence attached to every bead.

Davis wants you to come to dinner.

I am on the 22nd[2] out of 24 stories, very shaky, nervous, and flabby.

Vty

CORVO

III

Hogarth Club,
175 Bond St, W.
Feast of St. Partridge [*1899*].

DEAR BAINBRIDGE,

You're a brick.

I'll come on Saturday, some time.[1]

I shan't be any trouble to amuse: because I want to shut myself up in a bedroom and write AND WRITE, eating

II
  [1] Laid down as the third letter in the Martyr Worthy Collection.
  [2] 'About the Insistence of Sangiuseppe.'

III
  [1] Bainbridge had arranged for Rolfe to come to 69 Broadhurst Gardens, Hampstead, where Bainbridge lodged with Mrs. Isabelle Griffiths, a 'discerning landlady' who, his mother had decided, was the woman 'out of the whole of London' to have charge of his 'destiny.' Rolfe went to 69 Broadhurst Gardens on Saturday, 23 September 1899 and immediately or soon thereafter occupied Mrs. Griffiths's attic room and continued to occupy it until she removed to 15 Cheniston Gardens, Kensington, in March 1904 and Rolfe went with her. See also the *Introduction* above.

bread and butter and drinking milk. I do more work that way.

Tell them to expect me on Saturday.

Davis sends you his love & hopes you'll come another night when I am here again.

Br Corvo

IV

69 [Broadhurst Gardens
Hampstead].
xi. Nov. MCMI.

Dear Bainbridge,

Of course I shall be delighted to see you.[1] Will you dine here Tuesday or Wednesday at 7.30 or 7? The sight of you would be good for sore eyes; for I am lonely and unhappy. I wonder why you are liked, and more, wherever you go; and I abhorred. But do come.

Vty

Frederick William Rolfe

N.B.   Remember please that I have taken up arms against Slaughter and am watching my opportunity to smash him.[2]

IV

[1] Bainbridge spent the final months of 1901 examining the effects of lead fumes on the countryside surrounding lead works throughout the British Isles. During this period, he returned to London from time to time.

[2] Rolfe believed Slaughter guilty of collusion and general mismanagement of his affairs in a quarrel with Grant Richards, publisher, over Rolfe's book *Chronicles of the House of Borgia*, London: Grant Richards, 1901. On 6 March 1901, Rolfe had dissociated himself from Slaughter in a letter to Richards.

V

69 [*Broadhurst Gardens*],

Hampstead.

XXVI. Dec. 1901.

DEAR BAINBRIDGE,

A day at the B.M. only enabled me to touch the fringe of the subject.[1] I have a list of Doctors and shall examine catalogue for works which they may have written on the subject. I was able to find no gov: reports whatever on *external* influence of lead, but some on internal which is not what you want.

I shall be there again tomorrow and will write result.

I am glad you are in clover. Don't overdo it though. I used to find that 4 or 5 days of it once a month were beneficial: but that more were maleficial. Very few people know when to stop.

I got rather wretched on Christmas Day, and went for a little walk which made me worse. I envied the happy fools behind the window curtains lighted up.

I will see about your shirts.

Scott-Hall[2] sent me a ritualistick Xmas card and a note saying 'I do trust you will make your Christmas Communion ! ! !' He's a parson.

[Vty

FREDERICK WILLIAM ROLFE]

V

[1] The effects of lead fume; see above, Letter IV. Bainbridge asked Rolfe to investigate the matter at the British Museum.

[2] William Edmund Scott-Hall, whom Rolfe first met in Oxford. Scott-Hall posed and served continuously as a priest of the Church of England for about twenty years without having been ordained. Numerous misdemeanours are alleged against him.

14

VI

69 [*Broadhurst Gardens,*
Hampstead].
xxviii. Dec. 1901.

Dear Bainbridge,

I have been at B.M. all day. In these two days, I have read
the Report[1] of which you have a copy with the Evidence of
witnesses; and from the last I extracted a list of 28 doctors and
chymists.

According to the catalogue, which I minutely searched, none
of these 28 have written anything on your subject.

None of the Librarians were able to give me a clue: and I
myself have found none under any of the heads which you gave
me, or indeed under any head.

I consulted the Ballard (ticket with particulars enclosed).[2] He
discourses on *Stinks* such as are produced from tanneries, soap
works, manure, and fried fish, and appears to be useless for
your purpose.

I am not at all satisfied with this result: and if you have come
across any fresh clues, I shall be glad to verify and trace them.

Or at any rate, if you like, I will go again and continue to
ransack; for in many other matters I have experienced the same
preliminary difficulties in 'striking oil'; but when once one has
struck there is a regular gush.

Write me fully and say what you wish. I have finished my
book[3] and a change of work would do me good.

Last Tuesday I sent you a registered letter to Station Hotel

---

[1] Not identified.
[2] A British Museum ticket dated 23 December 1901 for delivery of *Report in
respect of the inquiry as to Effluvium Nuisances arising in connexion with various
manufacturing and other branches of industry*, London, 1882, by Edward Ballard,
M. D. to Frederick, Baron Corvo at Seat B5. On the reverse of the ticket,
Rolfe has written, 'Reprint of Report in Suppl. to Sixth Ann. Rep. of Loc.
Gov. Board in 1878.'
[3] *Don Renato An Ideal Content*, London: Francis Griffiths, 1909 (a suppressed
edition; the first published one was issued by Chatto & Windus in 1963).

containing Harland's[4] Xmas present, a cheque for two guineas, for which I asked you to send me cash as I have no other means of getting it. As I haven't heard from you since I'm afraid the letter reposes at Station Hotel. Do get it and remit, for I'm dying for a Turkish Bath.

Vty

F. W. R.

VII

[69 *Broadhurst Gardens,*
Hampstead].
xxxi. Dec. 1901.[1]

DEAR BAINBRIDGE,

Thanks for your cheque, received, cashed, dispersed. Let me know about my Noxious fumes letter. Give me a little more information, and if there is anything to be discovered at B.M. I will find it.[2]

Please write this letter on as swagger paper as you have handy. Put it into an envelope as much like enclosed as possible (in any case put it into an envelope which has not the maker's or stationer's name), and address it to

FREDERICK BARON CORVO,
c/o GRANT RICHARDS,
PUBLISHER,
LONDON.

VI

[4] Henry Harland (1861-1905) American born novelist, short story writer and an important part of the aesthetic movement in England, where he helped found and edit *The Yellow Book*. He was also associated with John Lane at the Bodley Head. Harland figures as Sidney Thorah in Rolfe's *Nicholas Crabbe*. There Rolfe tells how he first met Harland, by going to visit him 'bus-wise' at John Lane's suggestion, early in 1899. Harland and Rolfe were estranged some time in 1901 over the dedication of *In His Own Image*, which Harland refused. They continued an uneasy relationship, but Rolfe never forgave him.

VII

[1] Transcribed from Bainbridge's *Twice Seven*, pp. 112-14. '

[2] Bainbridge commissioned no further research at the British Museum. He did, however, ask Rolfe to revise the rough draft of the report made on completion of the tour of inspection. See *Appendix*.

Then post it in Newcastle.[3]

The Prince is much perturbed by your continued exile and silence; and, conceiving that you may once more have reduced yourself to penury the better to acquire certain information, His Excellency wishes me to inform you in this manner that 1,000 is at your call in the usual place together with a letter from H. E. who has read your book and has no other means of reaching you.

Allow me to add that H. E. is troubled by restlessness at night, the cause of which I imagine to be your immense sacrifice; and I venture to suggest that, if you could see your way to relax the rigour of your life for a month or two, and show H. E. that your health and spirits continue to be unimpaired, it would allay his extreme anxiety.

The yacht is leaving Tynemouth and proceeding N. and (via Canal if possible) to Glasgow, where the matter of Leo Neri mentioned in your last will receive minute investigation.

> H. C. BAINBRIDGE,
> 2, ST. THOMAS' CRESCENT,
> NEWCASTLE-ON-TYNE.

Then, write a duplicate of that and address it to

> FREDERICK BARON CORVO,
> c/o E. P. DUTTON,
> PUBLISHER,
> NEW YORK, U.S.A.

Post it also in Newcastle.

(He is G.R.'s agent in America. On receiving it he will send it to G.R. Complications will arise!)

I haven't the faintest idea what it all means. But, if anyone except you or I shall open these letters, they will have something to speculate about. I see the seeds of a romance in this.

I shall send you another letter to post in Glasgow, and another in Bristol.[4]

Happy New Year.

Vty

F. W. R.

VII

[3] Where Bainbridge was making inspection of lead works before going on to Glasgow and then to Bristol.

[4] If Rolfe sent the letters they are lost. In any case, Bainbridge did not post Rolfe's letters from Newcastle, as requested.

VIII

69 Broadhurst Gardens,
Hampstead. [1]

DEAR BAINBRIDGE,

Awfully sorry to worry you but can you make it a fiver by
return of post. It's desperate.

Vty

R

IX

[69 Broadhurst Gardens,
Hampstead]
Tuesday. [1]

DEAR BAINBRIDGE,

Many thanks. I instantly rushed out and wallowed in a
Turkish Bath.

Do come and see me when you will: but try to give me a day's
notice; and don't come on Friday. [2]

Vty

R.

VIII
[1] Laid down as the thirtieth letter in the Martyr Worthy Collection. This
and subsequent letters showing this address are written on light blue paper with
the address printed in black at the top of the left side.

IX
[1] Laid down as the thirty-first letter in the Martyr Worthy Collection.
[2] Since early 1902, Rolfe had devoted each Friday evening to his family and
especially his father, James Rolfe, who lived at 5 Highbury Hill. The elder
Rolfe was suffering from his last illness.

X

v. Nov. 1902.[1]

DEAR BAINBRIDGE,

I am sorry you did not come to lunch today.

With regard to the Kemmler Piano which you want, I find that, if you like to purchase it through my firm, I can get you a discount of 25% or 30% off the list price, according to the proportion of your cash—to your subsequent quarterly payments. And if the transaction were wholly a cash one, the discount allowed would be higher.

If you are in earnest about this make me a definite offer of a sum down and a proposal for subsequent quarterly payments.

I will then arrange for Jenkins[2] to go with you to inspect the instrument which you have chosen, and to give you the best advice procurable as to its quality and durability.

Then, if you decide to purchase, I will offer you the best terms.

Faithfully yours

FRED. WILL. ROLFE
for William Rolfe and Sons.

X

[1] Written on the letter head of William Rolfe & Sons, Pianoforte Manufacturers, of 5 Highbury Hill, London. This letter head represents a part of Rolfe's futile attempt to salvage something for his mother and sister from the remnants of the once prosperous family business after his father's death. James Rolfe had died in June 1902.

[2] Not traced. The only fact known about him is that he was a piano-tuner employed by the Rolfe firm. In *Hadrian the Seventh* (London: Chatto & Windus, 1904), p. 43, Rolfe described Jenkins as 'a venerable shy drudge of a piano-tuner whose left arm was dragged down by the weight of the unmistakable little bag of tools . . .'

XI

viii. Nov. 1902.[1]

DEAR BAINBRIDGE,

I send drafts of two letters which you should write, sign, & send, me at once. Then, if my arrangements work out right the piano will come to you on Thursday. I propose to come with it to collect your money: but will write you news again on Wednesday.

Faithfully yours,

FRED. WILL. ROLFE

DEAR ROLFE,

I am willing to buy of your Firm the Kemmler piano No 3856 of which I have spoken to you. There is no question of my buying it through the recommendation or intervention of any one besides yourself.

Faithfully yours

(HCB)

DEAR ROLFE,

I am willing to purchase of your firm the Kemmler piano No 3856 and I promise to pay you Twenty Pounds Cash on delivery of the instrument at my house and Three Pounds quarterly thereafter until the price is paid—the said price to be by mutual agreement as much under Thirty Three Guineas as you are able to allow me in justice to yourself after procuring the best terms possible from Messrs Kemmler: but in no case is the price to exceed Thirty Three Guineas.

Faithfully yours

(HCB)

XI
[1] Written on the letter head of William Rolfe & Sons. 8 November 1902 was a Saturday.

XII

69 Broadhurst Gardens,
Hampstead.[1]

DEAR BAINBRIDGE,

I have bought the piano 3856, and have paid for it. *It will
reach your place at 1 pm. Saturday.* You can now send me your
£20 on a/c. Perhaps I will come to you Sat. Eve to Monday
if convenient. I shall have to charge you a guinea for carriage
which is what they charge me. This is a private letter in haste
to relieve your mind.   Vty   F.W.R.

My humble duty to your charming family.

XIII

DEAR BAINBRIDGE,[1]

Enclosed I send Receipt for Twenty Pounds on account with
agreement for your signature as to the remainder. I don't know
whether you care to pay the carriage now. If you do, it will
be as well. If not add it to the last instalment. I should like to
send the assigned agreement to my sister as soon as possible.

Faithfully yours

FRED. WILL. ROLFE[2]

Received of M[r] H. C. Bainbridge the sum of Twenty Pounds
on account of Thirty Three Guineas, being price of Kemmler
Piano No 3856 Delivered Nov. 22. 1902.[3]

XII
  [1] Bainbridge wrote across the upper left corner, 'Cheque for £20 sent to
Rolfe 21/11/02' and, at the right of the inside address, 'Rec.[d] 21/11/02.'
XIII
  [1] The letter and each of the two enclosures are written on the letter head of
William Rolfe & Sons.
  [2] Below line drawn under Rolfe's signature, Bainbridge wrote, 'Agreement
signed & sent to Rolfe at 69 Broadhurst Gardens 25/11/02. *HCB*'.
  [3] With stamp across which Rolfe wrote, 'Twenty Pounds William Rolfe and
Sons Fred. Will. Rolfe Nov 22. 1902.'

Further instalments due:

xxii Feb. 1903. £3.

xxii May 1903. £3.

xxii Aug. 1903. £3.

xxii Nov. 1903. £3.

xxii Feb. 1904

In addition to the Twenty Pounds which I already have paid for the Kemmler Piano No 3856, delivered to me Nov. 22, 1902, I promise to repay to Miss N. E. Rolfe of 5 Highbury Hill, London, N, a further sum of Fourteen Pounds and Thirteen Shillings, bringing the price of the instrument up to Thirty Three Guineas, with One Guinea extra for carriage. Payment is to consist of quarterly instalments of Three Pounds each until the whole sum of Thirty Three Guineas and One Guinea is paid, and is to be due on the following dates viz. xxii Feb. 1903, xxii May 1903, xxii Aug. 1903, xxii Nov. 1903 and the balance on xxii Feb. 1904.[4]

XIV

69 Broadhurst Gardens,

Hampstead.

xi. Dec. 1902.

DEAR BAINBRIDGE,

I am quite done now. Which will perhaps explain my distrait air last night. I tried to canceal it as best I could.

Lane has given me a promise to publish the Rubai'yat early in January.[1] I have those 24 articles accepted by the Monthly

XIII

[4] Bainbridge signed, 'Henry Charles Bainbridge,' drew a wavy line and below it wrote, 'Nov. 25th 1902'.

XIV

[1] *The Rubáiyát of 'Umar Khaiyám Done Into English from the French of J. B. Nicolas,* London: John Lane The Bodley Head, 1903. At the suggestion of Temple Scott, an assistant of John Lane, and with the encouragement of Henry Harland and Kenneth Grahame, Lane had commissioned Rolfe to translate *The Rubáiyát* for £25. He began work on it early in 1900 and, as agreed, delivered it in May (23 May 1900) for July publication. Only after innumerable delays, evasions, and threats on Rolfe's part to appeal to the Society of Authors, Lane published the book on 26 January 1903 in New York and 27 February 1903 in London.

Review.[2] And two completed books to follow.[3] But I have no means of living and no place to live in till I get payment for this work. I have just 8/- left, no prospect of more, and not a soul in the world to help me. Indeed it would be a big job to help me now, after so long.

Think as kindly as you can of me, whatever you may hear said of me in future. I have tried my best and I have fail'd.

Always truly yrs

F. W. R.

XV

69 Broadhurst Gardens,

Hampstead.

xxvi. Dec. 1902.

DEAR BAINBRIDGE,

Thanks for your letters. I expected you on Thursday. I hope your illness is not serious.[1]

If I don't find a lump of money soon i.e. at once, we shall be sold up here and go to the workhouse. That is *literally* true.

The only thing is my Borgia Genealogy.[2] That is unique. No

XIV

[2] 'Reviews of Unwritten Books' of which *The Monthly Review* published only nine. The nine 'Reviews' were written by Sholte Douglas and revised and sold by Rolfe. Douglas declared that he received the entire fee paid for them, that Rolfe took none of it. For evidence to the contrary, see below Letters XVIII and XIX.

[3] *Don Renato* (see above, Letter VI, n 3) and *The Songs of Meleager*, London: The First Editions Club, [1937].

XV

[1] Bainbridge was ill with lead poisoning.

[2] A document $5\frac{1}{2}' \times 9\frac{1}{2}'$ originally prepared in a shorter form for inclusion in *Chronicles of the House of Borgia*, 1901 (see above, Letter IV, n 2) but deleted by Grant Richards. Thereafter the genealogy was Rolfe's hope and his obsession. He offered it on terms similar to those stated above to various people including William W. Astor, Victor Emmanuel III of Italy by way of his ambassador Alberto Pansa, the literary agent James Pinker, Dr. James Walsh of New York, and in 1913 Francesco Borgia and his son Cesare.

one else in the world has carried the history of the family so far. The last man collected 82 names. I have 293.

I want one of two things:-

(α) Some one who will buy the great chart from me, as a historical curiosity, as it stands. The price is £600.

(β) Some one who will finance me while I write the complete history of the Borgias on the lines of my Genealogy, i.e. using the Genealogy as the skeleton of a book which will be the Standard European work on the subject. In return for such assistance I will place the said patron's name on the book as co-author, and will make over to him the half of all profits issuing from its sale.

The only thing you can do in the matter is to broach the subject to some of the influential people known to you, to get them to see me and my work and to hear what I have to say about it.

There is the opportunity of winning both fame and money by such a work. The only reason why I do not do it by myself is my extreme poverty which keeps me from making use of my discoveries.

I have tried to put the thing concisely and clearly, and I think you will understand the position in which I stand. What is going to be done must be done without a moment's delay, for my ship is sinking fast.

So do what you can, now, please.

Faithfully yours

FRED. WILL. ROLFE

N.B. I can show praises of my work from *experts*, such as D[r] Garnett[3] of Brit. Mus. & People at Oxford.[4]

---

[3] Richard Garnett (1835-1906), English author and librarian, who had retired in 1899 as Keeper of Printed Books at the British Museum.

[4] Possibly Horace Hart, Comptroller of Oxford University Press and E. G. Hardy (1852-1925) of Jesus College.

XVI

DEAR BAINBRIDGE,

I suppose you're as hard up as I am, or else I should ask you
for some cash.

I've got to that point now when I am simply paralyzed for
want of about a couple of pounds worth of writing materials,
besides other things.

The result is that I'm losing the ground I have gained. By
rights I ought to keep on plugging away.

Of course any day I may get good news about my book[2] or
about the score of other M.S. which I have under consideration
of editors and publishers.[3]

But meanwhile I ought not to be idle a moment.

I feel like a beast to write this to you: but I must say it to
somebody. Or burst. Don't take any notice of it if you don't
like. I know how you feel; and how you are; and I shan't think
hardly of you anyhow.

Vty

R.

XVI

[1] Laid down as the twenty-ninth letter in the Martyr Worthy Collection.

[2] *Don Renato* (see above Letter VI, *n* 3).

[3] Throughout the last months of 1902 and much of 1903, Rolfe was reviewing
for *The Outlook.* He doubtless refers here, however, to original pieces not
definitely traced. Among them may be 'Notes on the Conclave,' *The Monthly
Review,* August 1903, pp. 74-88; 'Suggestion for a Criterion of the Credibility
of Certain Historians,' *The Westminster Review,* October 1903, pp. 402-14;
'Esoteric Jewellery;' 'Thirty Naughty Emperors;' and *The Songs of Meleager* (see
above Letter XIV, *n* 3).

XVII

69 Broadhurst Gardens,
Hampstead.
xiii. Feb. 1903

DEAR BAINBRIDGE,

Nothing has happened up to the time of writing, except another violent nerve-shattering scene this morning.[1] Summonses keep pouring in. God knows what will be the next move. The suspense is horrible.

Don't go any further with your scheme of having me at Bushey Heath.[2] *That is quite impossible.* During these years here I have been wearing out my under-clothes. Shirts, socks, boots, handkerchieves and everything, all are in rags and tatters. I can just manage to present *outwardly* a decent appearance about once a week not more. As long as I am here that will do. But you see that I cannot possibly move from here, and expose my nakedness in any decent house. Then again my books, papers, & tools of trade would have to be moved at a cost of some pounds if I am to do any more work.

No. Leave things as they are. When the worst comes, it must be faced. That's all. *I don't mind if you tell your people all about my affairs.* Your dear Mother spoke so kindly to me last night. But do not on any account pass any suggestion of bringing me to Bushey without stamping it out. It's good of you and delightful to me to think of it: but it is utterly impracticable. I was walking about town all day yesterday, trying to get an advance on my work without damaging my prospects by disclosing the real state of affairs. I had no success; and I am tired to death.

Vty

R.

XVII
[1] With his landlady Mrs. Griffiths.
[2] Shapwick, Bushey Heath, Herts., where Bainbridge lived with his mother and sisters.

XVIII

69 Broadhurst Gardens,

Hampstead.

xviii. Feb. 1903.

DEAR BAINBRIDGE,

She[1] has got the tax people to refrain from putting in a distress till end of the week.

Things remain just as hopeless as ever with me. I cannot get hold of any ready money anywhere at all.

The effort of keeping up a calm and frivolous appearance before these men is killing my power to write. I'm sure I shall go cranky all of a sudden.

Vty

R.

XIX

69 Broadhurst Gardens,

Hampstead.

Thursday [26 February 1903].

DEAR BAINBRIDGE,

She[1] says three judgment summons must be paid to-morrow Friday Amount £10. Can you lend me that? I'll give you a lien on the Reviews of Unwritten Books from which £15 will come in March and more later.[2]

Post it tonight please.

Vty

R

XVIII
    [1] Mrs. Griffiths.
XIX
    [1] Mrs. Griffiths.
    [2] From *The Monthly Review*, where the first of the 'Reviews of Unwritten Books' appeared in February 1903 and two appeared in each of the next four issues of the periodical.

XX

69 Broadhurst Gardens,
Hampstead.
iii. Mar. 1903.

DEAR BAINBRIDGE,

Thanks for sending cheque to my sister.[1] They are in a dreadful state there. My Mother has collapsed at last. D[r] says nothing but 6 months rest away from all worry will restore her. She can't move; and I watch her going mad from week to week.

G.[2] kèpt the baliffs out with a post-dated cheque. Just after it was due, I got an instalment from the Monthly Review: which met it and left me naked. That's all. It will happen again and again. With a lump of money I can make half a dozen fortunes out of the material I have. Without it I can do nothing.

Vty

R.

XXI

69 Broadhurst Gardens,
Hampstead.
v. Jun. 1903.

DEAR BAINBRIDGE,

I am sorry to write to you again about the over-due instalment.[1] You know that my sister invested the whole of her

---

XX
   [1] Rolfe has written in pencil above the first line and opposite the salutation: 'i.e. £3 re piano see receipt.'
   [2] Mrs. Griffiths.

XXI
   [1] Accompanying this letter is a receipt written on William Rolfe & Sons' letterhead in the hand of Nellie E. Rolfe. It reads: 'Received of H. Bainbridge Esq[re]. the sum of Three Pounds, Second Quarterly Instalment for Kemmler Piano due to me May 22nd 1903. With thanks. Nellie E. Rolfe [written over the stamp] June 9th 1903.'

savings;[2] and the non-appearance of the quarterly instalments at the regular time is a very serious matter to her.

Your continued silence also in regard to the March tuning involves trouble.

And I myself have been expecting to see you since your letter of *May 13th*.

Vty

ROLFE

XXII

[*69 Broadhurst Gardens,

Hampstead*].[1]

xxviiii. Aug. 1903.

DEAR BAINBRIDGE,

I beg to say that the Third Instalment of Three Pounds became due to my sister on the Twenty Second of August.[2]

Faithfully yours

FRED. WILL. ROLFE

XXI

[2] Nellie Rolfe later declared that such 'savings were *simply non existent.*' See Nellie E. Rolfe to David Roth, Worthing, 1 September 1955.

XXII

[1] Written on a post card imprinted with the name and address of William Rolfe & Sons.

[2] Accompanying this card is a receipt written on plain paper in the hand of Nellie E. Rolfe. It reads, 'Received of H. C. Bainbridge Esqre the sum of Three Pounds being the third instalment of the Kemmler piano bought of Messrs W. Rolfe & Sons November 22nd 1902. Nellie E. Rolfe [written over the stamp] Sept. 3rd 1903.'

XXIII

This is not private

69 Broadhurst Gardens,
Hampstead.
iiii. Sept. 1903.

DEAR BAINBRIDGE,

I had your letter and stay'd in for you. This is the third time in succession that you have led me to expect a visit, which you have fail'd to pay. If you do not desire my acquaintance, I wish you would declare the fact and come to a conclusion.

I am sorry to hear that things have not been going well with you. They have been going damnably with me; and, (as I have told you over and over again,) things will continue to go damnably with me as long as I am prevented from going on working.[1]

I wonder that you have not realized this fact; and that you have not once accepted my offer to join forces. Give me a chance to continue writing, and I shall be able to keep the whole lot of you; and my mother and sister as well, handsomely. But all through this year I have been harassed with threats of expulsion and even now I may be made homeless *at any moment*.

I have a lot of work, all the same.[2] If that is to be any good, I must continue to write, and keep myself before the public.

XXIII

[1] On 13 May 1903, The Royal Literary Fund had refused Rolfe's application for assistance. On 3 July 1903, Henry Newbolt had notified Rolfe that *The Monthly Review* would publish no more of his 'Reviews of Unwritten Books' and returned to him the fifteen which they still held. On 13 August 1903, Rolfe had discovered that his landlady Mrs. Griffiths and Henry Newbolt were in correspondence about Rolfe's prospects and that Newbolt had described them as very slight, a fact which discouraged Mrs. Griffiths's trust in her lodger. On 17 August 1903 Rolfe had learned that the Committee of the Royal Literary Fund had refused his May application because they suspected him of 'fraudelent misrepresentation' and he had then sorrowfully withdrawn a new application intended for consideration in October.

[2] The year 1903 is noteworthy in that by mid-March the first draft of *Hadrian the Seventh*, London: Chatto & Windus, 1904, was written and by July 12 the book was in final form.

Presently I shall make a success. Then all the back work which I have done will become hugely profitable.

But I cannot go on unless I have a place to write in, and peace. And, if I do not go on writing now, all my past work will be wasted.

I make a little ready cash now and then,[3] otherwise I should have died long ago. I would gladly give my earnings, as they come in, to any one who would house and feed me until I hit the bull's eye by indomitable perseverance. And, when I do become successful, I should know how to reward those who have enabled me.

As it is, you and I do not trust each other; and we are both in a bad way; and we shall both continue to go down and down, instead of up and up, simply because we work separately instead of together—simply because we do not join forces. So energy and opportunity is wasted. It is a great pity.

I have spoken.

Yrs

R

Return enclosed.[4]

XXIV

[69 Broadhurst Gardens,

Hampstead.]

vii. September 1903.[1]

DEAR BAINBRIDGE,

I was sorry to miss you; and I have your letter. If you hope to see me, you must give me notice and come this week: for I am

---

[3] In addition to the nine 'Reviews of Unwritten Books' published that year, Rolfe was paid for four reviews in *The Outlook*, 'Notes on the Conclave,' which appeared in *The Monthly Review*, August, pp. 74-78, and 'Suggestion for A Criterion of the Credibility of Certain Historians,' published in *The Westminster Review*, October, pp. 402-14. See above Letters XIV, XVI, XIX, and XX; below, Letter XXV.

[4] Not traced.

XXIV

[1] Transcribed from Bainbridge's *Twice Seven*, pp. 101-02.

wasting time, doing no work at all, with all my things packed up ready to go, living from hand to mouth, and running about frantically scratching up bare means to keep alive and sheltered.

All this is fatuous futile fatal rot. I ought to be writing continuously; and every day which is lost, in this brutally bestial hunt for a living, puts me a month further from the solid foundation which I already have laid. I ought to be building; and I am beating the air.

A swimmer in the Serpentine yesterday took his puppy into the water. Puppy wanted shore—swam to it—swimmer caught puppy and carried it further and further out—puppy's paws, though lifted right out of water, pattered and pattered in the action of swimming, but carried it no nearer shore, for the strong grip of swimmer rendered the pattering null and void of effect.

I resemble the puppy. I *must* patter most energetically towards the shore of success, but circumstances grip me, make my vigour vain, and carry me away. As long as this goes on, so much the longer will it be before I get to shore; and the chances are that I shall collapse.

It is hard to make you understand, because you all give me credit for being deep and abstruse instead of transparent and simple—because you all persist in reading *between* [instead of *on*]² the lines.

However: I always mean precisely what I say, and say precisely what I mean. Shew this and my last letter to your Mother. She read me correctly that night when she and your sister dined with the odious . . .³

But if you want to see me you must come this week and give me notice of your coming. My way is clear till Friday. Thence onward there is dense fog.

Vty.

R.

XXIV
² Rolfe's square brackets.
³ Bainbridge's omission.

32

XXV

69 Broadhurst Gardens,

Hampstead.

xii. Sept. 1903.

DEAR BAINBRIDGE,

You are very good. I can't come today, nor for a few days, because I have just got the proofs of a big thing accepted by Westminster Review.[1] These must be corrected and seen through the press at once; and there are also other things which detain me here. But let me know when you are coming to town; and let us meet. Meanwhile, if I can manage it, I will come out to you one day middle or end of next week.

Vty

R

XXVI

69 Broadhurst Gardens,

Hampstead.

xviii. Sept. 1903.

DEAR BAINBRIDGE,

I send six brief horoscopes.[1] Let them be read, marked, learned, and inwardly digested.

I think it will be best to send my things and come to you on

XXV

[1] 'Suggestion for A Criterion of the Credibility of Certain Historians.' See above, Letter XXIII, *n* 3. This article is a revised version of Appendix III to *Chronicles of the House of Borgia*, deleted by Grant Richards over Rolfe's strong protest.

XXVI

[1] A horoscope for Bainbridge, his mother, and each of his four sisters. All but Bainbridge's are lost. It reads,

Aug. 24th   The Lion

The vital person. Independent, *frank, fearless,* magnanimous, sincere, *rather proud,* determined, *strong-willed.* A generous enemy. Has the *constructive faculty.* Can be merry. Liable to rheumatism. Occultism will play an important part in life. Will succeed twice: once in middle life, and once later. Lucky stone, diamond. Metal, gold. Colour, orange. Important day, Sunday.

Monday. The sooner I begin to write, the sooner I sh'all be able to pay. The longer I remain here, the more time is wasted doing nothing profitable. Please lend me as much as you can manage, to effect the move. I am in such tatters that I cannot go into a decent house. Say four pounds. I will give you all I earn, as it comes in, to repay you for the convenience.

If it should so happen that you want to let Shapwick[2] while I am there, the obvious course will be to let it to me. But the future is on the knees of the gods. The present necessity is all we need attend to; and it seems plain that I must come to you and begin to use my undoubted abilities now running loose.

Vty

ROLFE

XXVII

Harry Bainbridge Shapwick Busheyheath Herts.[1]
Please come instanter fatal complications arising.[2]

ROLFE

XXVIII

69 Broadhurst Gardens,

Hampstead.

xxii. Sept. 1903.

DEAR BAINBRIDGE,

It seems that you do not understand. *Every hour wasted means a week's delay in getting money.*

I had everything packed, and was ready to leave on Monday morning and come to you and get to work. But I had just 6ᵈ and

---

XXVI
  [2] The Bainbridge residence; see above, Letter XVII, *n* 2.

XXVII
  [1] Telegram handed in at Finchley Road at 9.45 a.m.; received at 10.49 a.m. The Bushey Heath office stamp shows 2.45 p.m. on 21 September 1903.
  [2] Mrs. Griffiths had again threatened Rolfe with eviction, insisting that he go with only the clothes he was wearing.

no more; and I expected something from you. (I want to give her[1] 30/-, and to pay carriage of my tools of trade, and to get one or two absolute necessaries.) Instead, I got your letter putting me off. On the top of that came a most violent scene with her. She was refusing to let me move my things.

Then I wired to you.

The day was a day of horrible abuse. I began to feel like going mad. I hadn't a penny. I was expecting you every minute. In the evening I asked her to let me wait till the last post. Then I would go and walk about till morning, and come again for my letters. She flung at me leave to stay for the night. I stayed and did not sleep a wink.

This morning I got your letter. I told her you were likely to come. I have been walking up and down the room all day. Now at 5.30 I am writing to say that I feel sure she will turn me out to-night. Never mind. I will keep alive. On Wednesday morning[2] I will come here again for my letters. Then I will continue to walk about near and call again at noon. And at night. I used to be able to go four days without food. I think I can do two now.

I am placing all my confidence on you. When you get this, for goodness' sake *wire* me some money and leave to come to you. Four pounds will just do.

Don't delay me a moment longer from my work.[3] Here I am fast going frantic from forced inaction. The sooner I begin to work again the sooner I shall recover my lost ground.

Or, if you prefer it, come here and fetch me. But the first is easiest and best for both of us.

Vty

R.

Burn this

XXVIII
[1] Mrs. Griffiths.
[2] The next day.
[3] Rolfe was probably beginning *Nicholas Crabbe*. See above, Letter I, *n* 2.

XXIX

69 *Broadhurst Gardens,*

Hampstead.

xxiiii. Sept. 1903.

DEAR BAINBRIDGE,

Your letter received. She won't listen to the proposal.[1] She is abominably rude. For God's sake come and see me as soon as ever you can. Depend upon it that I will stick here, even though I go raving mad in the process, until I am turned-out.

Meanwhile this I beg. Give me leave to send my things to you and store them in your stable until I can come or can claim them.

This morning I have got 8/6 from the Outlook.[2] I am going to try to call you up on the telephone to say this in order to save time. Then I am going to have my boots repaired and to get some tobacco and to continue writing.

I reiterate that the 'anxiety and trouble' which excruciates both of us will continue until I am free to manoeuvre for both of us.

XXX

[69 *Broadhurst Gardens,*

Hampstead.

24 September 1903.][1]

This is the best plan. Get me a bed-sitting-room, as near your place as possible, *and wire for me to bring myself & baggage at*

XXIX

[1] Mrs. Griffiths; the details of the proposal are unknown.

[2] For 'Microcosmic Macedonia,' an anonymous review of *Macedonian Folklore* by G. F. Abbot in *The Outlook*, 5 September 1903, p. 134.

XXX

[1] Written on a blue-green letter-card postmarked 25 September 1903 at 1.00 a.m. at Watford.

once. Tell the people I'm an author who wants to be quiet and write a book. Make yourself responsible to them. All I get shall be handed to you.

Then, when you have room for me at Shapwick I can come in there.

I can just manage to get to Stanmore (if I can come within 24 hours) with the Outlook money.[2] I shall send the baggage by Parcels delivery and it can be paid there.

But let me get out of this instantly.

XXXI

[*69 Broadhurst Gardens,*
Hampstead.
28 September 1903.][1]

I am sorry you had the trouble of coming with the books.[2] They were sent to Shapwick because I notified the editor of the Outlook of my change of address on the strength of your promise.

I am sorry you had the trouble of waiting $2\frac{1}{2}$ hours. After waiting 6 days, I took the liberty of going out but I should have stayed in if you had sent the necessary warning.

As you will not take in my belongings of course I must be content to lose my work and tools of trade.

As you will not give me personally a chance,—the last and only—there is nothing before me but the workhouse.

Ta ta

XXX
[2] See above, Letter XXIX.

XXXI
[1] Written on a blue-green letter card postmarked 28 September 1903.
[2] Books sent to Rolfe for review.

XXXII

69 Broadhurst Gardens,
Hampstead.
xiii. Oct. 1903.

DEAR BAINBRIDGE,

A certain farmer formerly went into his poultry-yard, saying 'Dear fowls, the time has come when we must settle with what stuffing you are to be stuffed.' The capon said in reply, 'But, sir, we do not desire to be cooked!' And the farmer answered him, 'Bird, you evade the point.'

There is no question about your bearing half my loss on the agreement for tuning your piano.[1]

At the present time you owe me 5/3 for one tuning; and you ought by rights to pay for the second tuning which you would not allow my representative[2] to do: but the latter is your affair, not mine.

It remains for you :-

(α) to explain, or apologize for, the unbusinesslike discourtesy of calling in another tuner during your agreement with me:

(β) to say whether you are going to keep your promise to let me know when to do the third tuning now long overdue:

(Γ) to decide whether you wish to break the agreement for four tunings now, or to afford me facilities for performing my part.

I am willing to meet your convenience in all things reasonable, now that you are in possession of facts: but you must understand that, (until you have broken your agreement with me, or until you have allowed me to perform my share,) I cannot recognize your right to give your custom to my trade-rival, or Messrs Kemmler's rights to poach (at your instigation) on my preserves. It is quite simple for you to send me the sum due

---

XXXII
[1] For details of Bainbridge's purchase of a piano see above, Letters X-XIII.
[2] Jenkins (see above, Letter X).

with a note saying that you wish to break your connection with me; and then I should inform Messrs Kemmler that the road was open to them.

But the present condition of things is 'not cricket.'

Faithfully yours

FREDERICK WILLIAM ROLFE
for William Rolfe and Sons

XXXIII

iiii. Nov. 1903.[1]

DEAR BAINBRIDGE,

In the event of your cousin[2] purchasing through me either of the two pianos which you today have selected at Brinsmead's, my charges to him will be a follows:

(α) *Forty-two Guineas* for the solid oak model 54349, which is listed at *Fifty-two Guineas:*

(β) *Forty Guineas* for the black model 54725, which is listed at *Forty-seven Guineas.*

These terms are *cash to me;* and your cousin would have to return the packing-case to Brinsmead at his own cost.

Faithfully yours

FREDERICK WILLIAM ROLFE
for William Rolfe and Sons

XXXIII
[1] Written on the letter head of William Rolfe & Sons.
[2] Not traced.

XXXIV

69 Broadhurst Gardens,
Hampstead.
iiii. Dec. 1903.

DEAR BAINBRIDGE,

I deplore impossibility.[1] Please furnish necessary lie for Brinsmead.

Faithfully yours

ROLFE

XXXIV
[1] The impossibility of Bainbridge's cousin purchasing a piano from Brinsmead through Rolfe (see above, Letter XXXIII.)

APPENDIX[1]

DEAR SIR,

in re Lead Fume[2]

As the reports, which I have sent you to the present date, are compiled in the main simply from evidence and opinions obtained by me from various people, you may consider it desirable that I myself should submit to you certain personal observations on this subject.

I. I have not seen a Leadworks which possesses all the necessary conditions as to situation and good condensation of fume.

Those situate in towns, where there is little or no vegetation[3] to be damaged, have the best condensation.

Those situate in the country may be divided into two classes:-

(1) where the output is small, and the condensing apparatus capable of dealing with a much larger quantity of fume than is emitted:

(2) where the output is larger, and the condensing apparatus inadequate.

Works situate in country districts smelt Lead Ores, and treat Ashes, and Lead Sulphate,—etc., only. I have not seen a works (manufacturing from pig-lead only) which is capable of doing damage to vegetation. Therefore, I incline to think that the effect of Sulphur fumes should be taken into consideration, as well as the effect of Lead fumes.

II. In all cases which have come under my notice, the owners of lead-smelting works situate in the country either own, or hold leases of, considerable tracts of land surrounding their works. For this reason, they are able to control hostility which may exist, and which does exist. It should be noted that the stacks of the greater number of these mills are situate on moorland, where no damage to agriculture is possible.

III. The mill most suitable for an enquiry[4] into the effects

---

[1] See above, Letter VII, *n* 2.

[2] Above these words Rolfe has written '("re" is absolutely ungrammatical)' and drawn an arrow pointing to these words.

[3] Substituted for the word agriculture through which Rolfe has drawn a line.

[4] Above this word Rolfe has written 'inquisition.'

of Lead on Land is situate at Castleside near Blackhill, Durham. Here, the position and condensation are all that could be desired. But there is only one Hearth at work smelting galena, etc.; and there is considerable length of flue, capable of dealing with larger quantities of fume. When I visited this mill, the Hearth was working, and no escaping vapour was visible. The owner tells me that he produces about 1300 tons of pigs legs per annum: but that when, formerly, he refined about 400 or 500 tons of rich lead, to obtain silver for some of the great Tyneside firms, he experienced no trouble from claims, and knew of no bad effects on animals or vegetation. From the fact that the condition of the surrounding country corroborates this statement, I am led to believe that 'chemical quantities' of lead cause no damage to vegetation. (By 'chemical quantities' I mean the small amount escaping from an efficient condensing apparatus.

IIII. Additional corroboration of this view may be obtained from the condition of the country surrounding the Lee Bridge Leadworks, Derbyshire; where there is a considerable escape of fume with less damage to vegetation than might be expected. I ought to say, however, that in this case the damage is due more to the fumes of sulphur than to those of lead.

V. At the same time if it be maintained that the amount of lead escaping from any chimney is insufficient to cause perceptible damage, there can be little doubt but that strong prejudice is likely to arise against any *new* Leadworks which may be established in the midst of a country district.

VI. Leadworks, which at present exist in country districts, are of long standing. Several generations of the inhabitants in their neighbourhood have obtained a livelihood to a great extent thereby; and, consequently, have found it to their interest to oppose no obstacles to their actual means of existence.

VII. But, if *new* Leadworks be erected in a district already possessing other sources of employment, the people will be likely to keep a sharper look-out for damage, than is the case in the vicinity of old-established mills.

VIII. Therefore, I submit that it will be more necessary to prove that no lead escapes, than to prove that no damage is done, especially if the new works be located in a district which supplies food for human consumption; i.e. we ought to be certain of our ability effectually to condense our fumes: or we ought to use some method of oxide manufacture where the fumes (if any) are emitted in inconsiderable volume.

VIIII. Further, if the present process of making Litharge be continued, the subsequent disposal of the fumes, in such a way as to avoid the production of acid fumes and lead dust, should be taken into consideration.

In this report, I have been obliged to depart at times from the actual subject of enquiry, viz. 'The Claims received by Existing Leadworks on a/c of Damage to external vegetation etc., caused by Lead'; because, in practically every case brought under my notice, there has been some qualifying statement or condition, which prevents the acquisition of a definite idea as to what the effect would be on a country district of Leadworks manufacturing only pig lead, turning out a large output, and using an adequate condensing apparatus.

INDEX

350 *copies of this book*
have been printed on Chariot Cartridge.
In addition there are 45 *copies*
on Basingwerk Toned Parchment
specially bound and numbered I to XLV.